500 Heartwarming Expressions

For Crafting, Painting, Stitching and Scrapbooking

by Sandy Redburn
Artwork by Suzanne Carillo and Shelly Ehbrecht

Crafty Secrets Publications
15430 78A Ave.
Surrey, B.C. Canada
V3S 8R4

ISBN 0-9699410-8-0   Printed in Canada

Table of Contents - Book 1

Themes for Border & Expression Pages

There is a smorgasbord of creative supplies and helpful aids for lettering expressions onto an almost endless array of surfaces. Check with your local retail stores for products from the manufacturers listed below.

Zig Memory Products
EK Success Ltd
PO Box 1141
Clifton, NJ 07014
www.eksuccess.com

Pigma® Ink Products
Sakura of America
30780 San Clemente St.
Hayward, CA 94544-7131
www.gellyroll.com

Needle Craft Alphabet and Design Books
ASN Publishing
1455 Linda Vista Drive
San Marcos, CA 92069
www.asnpub.com

Oil Pencils, Woodburning Tools, Blank Wood Pieces
Walnut Hollow Farm. Inc.
1409 State Road 23
Dodgeville, WI 53533-2112
www.walnut@walnuthollow.com

Introduction

Here we are back with our new revised Book #1, from the Heartwarming Expressions series. Previously titled 425 Heartwarmin' Expressions, this first of three books now includes over 500 Heartwarming Expressions along with 40 new border pages!

From the beginning the goal was to create a fun, versatile book that could be used for a wide variety of craft and hobby interests, skills and mediums. Those with limited creative skills can relax. You don't need a lot of talent or money to put this book into action. The craft, scrapbook and sewing industries all overflow with innovative and easy to use supplies and techniques to suit every style and budget. By using pens and markers, a paint brush or needle and thread, you can add expressions to all kinds of creative projects. You likely already have some bare surfaces waiting to be transformed into a sentimental family treasure, or a whimsical feel good statement.

Thanks Are Due

There were many people involved in the creation of this book and they deserve a big round of applause and thank you! Thanks to every creative soul who passed on their favorite expressions. To Diane at Splash Graphics and Claire Patterson at Webcom for their hard work. Thanks to my family for their ongoing patience and support, while I spent many months in our dining room in an "endless paste-up party", fitting all the expressions and artwork onto each page. I love doing some of the lettering but I saved all the fancy lettering and artwork for Suzanne and Shelly. So, the biggest thank you must go to them, because their talented hard work has added special personality to every page in this book.

Also, a big heartwarming thanks to YOU for buying this book. Have great fun spreading smiles!

Sandy

Sandy Redburn's dedication to inspiring others' creativity includes writing, publishing and teaching seminars since 1993. As the author of the Heartwarming Expressions Books, Sandy admits to being addicted to creating new expressions but promises to stop now at 500 (actually this book has over 500). She owns three rhyming dictionaries and also loves to use great quotes from Miss Piggy to Shakespeare. She runs her successful home-based business with the help of her husband and three daughters.

Shelly Ehbrecht's speciality is in her wonderful lettering and she has contributed greatly to this book from its birth, helping to make it all possible. Shelly has received her CPD, (Certified Professional Demonstrators Diploma) and enjoys teaching folk art painting classes. She is also a full time registered nurse on a maternity ward and lives a happy and busy life with her husband and two daughters.

Suzanne Carillo is a multi-talented artist who was brought on board in 1999 to help with the illustrations and artistic lettering in this book. Now in this revised edition Suzanne's whimsical and humorous artwork and hand lettering grace so many pages, her name has been added to the cover. Suzanne works as a freelance artist.

Easy Lettering Tips & Tricks

Lettering is not as hard as you may think and, as you will see throughout this book, by no means does it have to be perfect or for that matter straight! You can do your lettering by free hand, or you can trace our expressions and designs right onto your project.

If you would like your lettering larger, you can recreate any expression using the enlarged alphabets in the back of this book. You may also photocopy any expressions and have them enlarged or reduced to fit your personal needs.

Trace or pencil on your lettering first, to get your spacing right. A good eraser and see-through plastic ruler are two very helpful tools for lettering.

It's Easy!

1. Use a pencil & ruler. Lettering does not have to be even - just consistent.
2. Hold pens in an upright position.
3. When possible pull your pen rather than push.
4. Add extra embellishments to create different styles.
5. Get bravely creative - but remember practice and patience.

Dot lettering is one of the easiest styles of printing to reproduce. Remember you do not have to embellish your letters with dots. As you will see, you can change your printing style by adding hearts, stars, flowers, snowflakes, holly, stitching lines and more!

There are countless design books available, with wonderful patterns you can incorporate with our expressions. Look around you for inspiration and be sure to read our list of *99 Places To Put An Expression* inside the front cover. Once you start, you will find life offers endless "perfect spots" to add a Heartwarming Expression or tickle some funny bones.

Using Pens & Markers

Using Pens and markers is easy and fun because they are now available in a multitude of tip styles, sizes and colors in both water based and permanent inks. Water based pens work well for a variety of paper crafts, but permanent pigma ink markers won't fade and can be used on a large variety of surfaces. The manufacturers of these markers all agree you should hold your pens in an upright position so the tip has full contact with the writing surface. It may feel a bit awkward but will give you the true essence of the pen tip.

You will also find you have better control of your pen when you pull it towards you rather than pushing it away.

Our samples below show how different combinations of pen tips can give your lettering lots of personality and style. They were done with black ink, so imagine adding colour. There are several helpful lettering books available, as well as computer software with fonts that look hand lettered.

Family

Letters - Pigma Graphic 3, Outline - Zig 08 Millennium
Stitches & Heart - Pigma Micron 03

Stitchin

Letters - Pigma Graphic 3
Stitch Lines - Pigma Micron 01

Hearts

Letters - Zig 08 Millennium
Hearts - Pigma Micron 01

Housework Stinks

Letters - Zig 08 Millennium
Embellishments - Pigma Micron 03

Life

Letters - Zig 08 Millennium
Shade - Pigma Micron 03

M♥M

Letters - Pigma Micron 01
Shade - Pigma Micron 05

Inspiration

Letters - Sakura Brush Marker
Dots - Pigma Micron 01
Snowflakes - Pigma Micron 03

Creative Possibilities

Photo copying
Our Designs & Border Pages

You can use the expressions and designs in this book as clip art to create album pages, cards, tags, magnets stationary and more. *You don't have to cut the pages of this book.* Please read our copyright restrictions on the first page of this book. For your personal use, have the designs you want to use enlarged or reduced on a good quality photocopier. From your copy, cut out the expression, graphics, border etc. and lay them out on a piece of paper. Attach them with a glue stick, removeable tape or rubber cement. Copy this page onto your final "good" paper or card stock, which you can decorate with colored pens or pencils. You can also have color copies made of your work. Color copies are perfect for scrapbooks, calenders and decoupaging onto projects. Many people prefer to use a light box and simply trace the design they want to use. Anything you want to save for years should be copied or traced onto acid free paper.

Transferring Tips

Depending on your project, you may want to transfer expressions and designs from this book. Once you decide on what you want to use, lay tracing paper over it and draw it out. Lay your traced design on your project surface and slip some transfer paper in between your design and prepared surface. Trace the outline with a stylus or empty pen tip. Saral®

manufactures a wax free transfer paper that works on wood, fabric, metal, glass, tile, ceramic, etc. Wax free paper will not clog the tips of your markers and pens. Heat activated transfer pencils also work well on fabric.

Expressions For Scrap booking & Paper Crafts

You can use our expressions to create your own special occasion and seasonal decorations, birthday cards, scrapbooks, framed calligraphy, greeting cards, gift tags, invitations, stationary and wrapping paper. Jazz up your projects with colored pencils and inks, watercolors, metallic markers, glitter pens, decorative punches and scissors, templates, stencils, stickers, rubber stamps, 3D or traditional decoupage, paper castings, ribbon and more! Again if you are creating anything you wish to preserve for many years use acid free supplies.

Expressions On Wood

If you don't have a steady hand for doing your lettering with a paintbrush, don't worry, you can cheat and use permanent markers. When you apply dots to letters on wood, use paint rather than your pen tip. Not only will you save the life of your pens, you can create dots faster and more consistent in size using paint. Dots can be made using a brush tip, stylus or embossing tool. We use corsage pins and various plastic headed pins for different size dots. Stick the pins into the eraser tip of a pencil and just dip the head into paint. When using permanent markers for lettering, test any varnish first. Krylon manufactures a Clear Matte Spray Finish, which won't make the ink in permanent markers bleed.

Expressions On Fabric

Pre-wash fabric to remove any sizing and don't use fabric softener. You can use a heat activated transfer pencil, or place some fabric transfer paper between your design and fabric (following all manufacturers' directions). Before painting your transferred design, place a piece of cardboard under your fabric surface (a cookie sheet will also work). Use fabric paints or regular acrylics mixed with a textile medium. Look for quality brushes recommended for textile painting, fabric markers, or use the mini tips on paint bottles to do lettering. You can also have a copy centre put your design onto transfer paper, which you can iron onto clothing, quilts, pillows and more. Remember any lettering must be mirrored or it will transfer backwards.

Expressions On Glass & Ceramics

Paint expressions on an assortment of dishware, tiles, glasses, vases and decor. You can use traditional ceramic techniques and glazes, or cheat and use the new glass and ceramic paints. We love the new paint liner pens which are great for lettering. These paints should be baked in an oven for a permanent finish.

Expressions By Needle & Thread

Stitching includes an array of techniques for applying expressions, using fancy threads, floss, yarns, ribbons or beads. Machine or hand embroidery, hand stitching on felt, needlepoint, cross stitch, plastic canvas, quilted appliqués and silk ribbon embroidery are all popular decorative embellishments. You can stitch expressions on everything from baby bibs to bumper pads, decorative pillows, wall samplers, aprons, linens, sweatshirts, vests, jumpers, jean jackets, boxer shorts, ties, bathrobes and more!

The American School of Needlework (ASN Publishing) is a great source for cross stitch design books. They have generously donated the cross stitch alphabets on page 87 in this book. If you don't want to stitch by hand, check out the amazing things you can create with an embroidery machine today!

Embellishing Your Expressions

Depending on the materials and style of your project you can also embellish expressions with raffia, jute, wire, paper twist, ribbons, lace, trims, buttons, charms, shells, fabric motifs, lace appliqués or miniature accessories. To add extra personality to a collection of dolls or stuffed animals, try creating some mini signs to add to the display. You are only limited by your imagination, so go on . . . get creative!

I ♥ Angels

Expect Miracles

ANGELS

Angels Gather Here

Angels can fly because they take themselves lightly

Listening Hearts Hear Angels Sing

Never Drive faster than Angels can FLY

Angel Collector

Angels light the way

When in doubt, Look up!

Angel Crossing

An Angel's Work is Never Done ☆

We Believe In Angels

ANGELS ON DUTY

An angel's heart is filled with love.

Earthly angels are... mothers in disguise

Angels sent from up above
Please protect the ones we love

Thanks you're a Real Angel!

9

Oh wide wonderful world with the beauty of nature around you curled and the mornings light painted across your breast, Oh world, you are so beautifully dressed

Bless this Home with Love

Lord,
Grant me the patience
to endure my blessings

Count your blessings
day by day
And all your cares
will fly away.

God is Love

May the Dear Lord
Bless and Keep you safe

Thou Shalt Not Whine

May God Keep You in His Care

Shalom means Everything

The Mennora the Merrier

Happy is ye Thankful Heart

Smile God Loves You

Bless This Country Home

A friend is a very special blessing

Thanks for all those little things
you always do and say
That make me feel so blessed
and happy each and every day

Life is precious handle with prayer

SWEET DREAMS
SLEEP TIGHT
GOD BLESS
GOODNIGHT

Blessings surround us every day
we just have to look the right way

11

Claus & Co.

Have Yourself a Merry Little Christmas

CHRISTMAS

Dear Santa: I want it ALL! xox

Show me the Presents!

The Very Best Gifts of All

Joy Faith Love PEACE

No HUMBUGS Allowed

Santa Claus Lane

WE BELIEVE IN SANTA

ELF*MADE

Just say Ho!

SANTA STOPS HERE

Just B___ claus

And to all a GOOD NIGHT

North Pole ↑
Brake for Reindeer

Frosty....
You melt
my heart.

Sleigh Parking

There's no people like SNOWPEOPLE

All other vehicles will be snowed

13

Jesus is the Reason for the Season

Let it snow

Let it snow

Let it snow

Christ is the best part of Christmas

Have a Heavenly Christmas

May the Magic of Christmas Shine in Your Heart

Peace Unto The World

Joy to the World

Christmas is for sharing and caring

We Believe

All Hearts Come Home For Christmas

May Your Christmas Be Bright and Full of Delight

Twinkle Twinkle Christmas Star

You put the Merry in my Christmas

15

From: Meow
To: You

LOVE ME
LOVE MY DOG

You're purr...r...fect

THE WELCOME WAGGIN'

WIPE YOUR PAWS

If you want the best seat
in the house
You'll have to move the cat

Forget the dog
BEWARE
of the KIDS!

Dogs
Laugh
with
their
Tails

Dogs think they are Human
Cats know they are

We had to get rid
of the kids
the cat was allergic

Blessed are the
PURR in heart

Cutie
Cat

THE ONLY
SELF CLEANING THING
IN THIS KITCHEN
IS THE CAT!

ATTACK CAT
ON DUTY

CATS
are for the
birds!

CAT'CHA
LATER

HAVIN' A ROOTIN'-TOOTIN' WING-DING TIME

EveryBunny is Welcome

COUNTRY CRITTERS

HOP ON IN

WHAT'S MOO WITH EWE?

Ewe are my sunshine

♥ Love ♥
one an-udder

Home is where your herd is

Every bird loves his own nest BEST!

I LOVE YOU
MOO AND MOO
EACH DAY

Waddle
I do
Without You?

BEWARE of STAMPEDES

SOMEBUNNY Loves you

Ewe's Wooly Wonderful

there's only one ewe

♥ EWE ARE LOVED ♥

It's ewe and me FOREVER

This ol' cowboy ain't out to pasture yet

All Dolled Up

Doll Collector at Heart

one can never have too many dolls

Dolls are like potato chips . . . .
You can't have just one.

The nicest dreams that will ever be... are the dreams shared by my dolly and me.

Some of my best friends are . . . . .
DOLLS

Dolly's blue...
Without You

I can hardly wait till night time falls when I crawl into bed with my favorite dolls

Discover your inner child —
Play with dolls!

I'm just a Raggedy Ann in a Barbie Doll World

Never too old to play with dolls!

Doll Crossing

Families are Forever

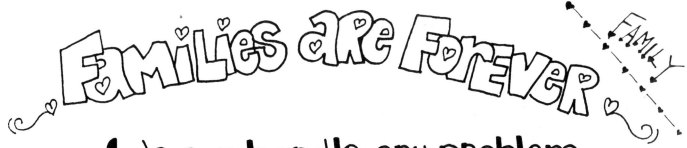

FAMILY

We can handle any problem
We have Kids

The best thing to spend on your children is TIME

Our family is a circle of love.

Childhood is a journey..... not a race.

Sisters by fate, Friends by choice.

Kid Crossing

Mothers of little boys work from SON up til SON down.

Children are like seeds..... Nurture them with love.

The Best Place To Be Is In A Loving Family

There's no better friend..... than a brother

Always my sister Forever my friend

A FAMILY IS A PATCHWORK OF LOVE

A Family Stitched Together with Love Seldom Unravels

FAMILY

Nana means Love

Grandma's Kitchen
KIDS EAT FREE!

Our Most Treasured Heirlooms Are Our Sweet Memories

Memories

Grandmas have the best hugs & cookies
X ⊙ X

Nana's the name and spoiling is the game

If Mom says NO!
call
1 ♥ 800 ♥ GRANDMA

Grandpa's fixin' shop

There's no place like home....... ♥ except Grandma's

Grandmas are.....
just antique little girls

Grandpas are just antique little boys

A Grandma is a Treasure of Memories 25

Babies are made in heaven.

Babies add so much love to life

Gods biggest treasures are his little ones

Thank heaven for.. babies little girls little boys

Babies are...... a miracle of LOVE

"A mother's love is like a melody "

God made you my MOM Love made you my FRIEND!

A mother's love grows FOREVER

A mother holds her children's hands for a little while ... and their hearts forever

Dad's the Boss Mom said

shhh....Dad's Sawing Logs

Anyone can be a father but it takes someone special to be a Daddy

To our children we can give two things ... the security of roots, the confidence of wings.

A Mother's Love is Tied with Heartstrings

Good Friends ♥ Good Food ♥ Good Times

FRIENDSHIP

When friends meet hearts warm

Together is the Nicest Place ~to be~

Rain or Shine You are a friend of mine

In the cookie of life, FRIENDS are the chocolate chips

FRIENDSHIP IS A RAINBOW BETWEEN TWO PEOPLE

You have to be a good friend to have one

Friends See heart to heart

Friendship is a treasure..... with a value beyond measure

Old Friends Make the Best Antiques

Little by little, day by day ... friends and flowers grow this way

Daisy

Rose

Between the houses of friends, the road is never long

Friends are flowers in life's garden.

29

Friends are hugs for the heart

FRIENDSHIP

Friendship is a Work of Heart

Even when we're 93
best friends we shall
always be

Neighbors
are side by side
FRIENDS

Friendship
is for
Sharing &
Caring

A FRIEND IS
A FOREVER THING

Good
friends
are
4 Keeps

A good friend is one
who comes in
when the whole world
goes out

Friends are always
at home
in our hearts

The seasons may come and go
but friends last forever

Nothing Warms the Heart Like a Friend

Friendship is the thread in the patchwork of life.

Friends become chosen Family

Let The Good Times Roll!

Let The Good Times Roll!

Laughter Prolongs Life

I'm not FAT...
I'm Fluffy

Some do Richard Simmons
I do Sara Lee!

Life is full of UPS and Pounds

Chocolate, Coffee and men...
Some things are just better when RICH!

Dieting is wishful shrinking

If there are no malls in heaven...
I'm not going!

A woman's place is in the mall

Money isn't everything...
But it sure keeps the kids in touch

When the going gets tough,
The tough go shopping

$pend til the end!

I can't be out of money
I still have checks left
(cheques)

Of all the things I've lost...
I miss my mind the most

33

Too Much of a Good Thing
is Wonderful -Mae West

Menopausal Maniac

Never eat
more than
you can lift
-Miss Piggy

Never go to bed MAD...
Stay up and fight. -Phyliss Diller

I am man
Hear me ROAR
(while I snore)

A Closed Mouth Gathers No Feet

HUSBAND
FOR SALE
TV and remote
included

Blondes prefer Gentlemen
-Mae West

Give me patience...but please hurry!

I'll stop procrastinating...
TOMORROW

If it weren't for the
last minute.....
nothing would get done

Marriages
are made in heaven...
so are thunder and lightning

If friends were noses...
I'd pick you

I've used up all my sick days...
Now I'm calling in dead......35

Garden Sweet Garden

Gardening angels plant seeds of Love

Cultivate a Gratitude Attitude

The Latest Dirt:

Earth Laughs In Flowers

Gardeners spread THE BEST DIRT!

Plant Kindness & Gather Some Love

Kindness

BLOOM where you're planted

Friends are flowers that never fade.

Life's a Peach

Plant seeds of trust row on row...
And you will see a friendship grow.

37

Fruit of the Bloom

YOU'RE ONE IN A MELON

If friends were carrots I'd pick you

GARDEN of WEEDIN'

Mom's Garden
Dad's Weeds

Bee My Honey

Welcome to Our Nest

You're Berry Sweet

I carrot about you a whole bunch

THANKS A WHOLE BUNCH

Scatter seeds of kindness .....wherever you go......

Gardening...... just another day at the plant...

BEWARE OF SNAP DRAGONS

Welcome to Our Patch

In MY Garden Love Grows

BEST WITCHES & HAPPY HAUNTING

MIND YOUR MUMMY

BAT MOM

BROOMS 4 SALE
Flying Lessons 10¢

HOME OF THE WICKED WITCH
AND ALL HER LITTLE MONSTERS

Off we go a-haunting

Broom Parking 5¢

BLOOD DONORS NEEDED
SEE THE COUNT

Forget the ghosts,
Beware of the
sugar bugs

Have a spooktacular
Halloween!

♥ You're no bunny 'til somebunny loves you. ♥

You Are Eggstra Special

Hoppy Easter

You're Egg...cellent!

41

No Smoking · Country Air

If you smoke –
leave your butt outside

Don't Smoke –
you might croak

*Good Planets are
hard to find*

Don't Worry
Bee Happy

It's a small world.........
let's live together in peace

Peace
is not a season
it's a way of life

You Are My Sunshine

*The most important
things in life
aren't things*

Fertilize Yourself
take your vitamins

Life by the yard
is hard
By the inch...
a cinch

43

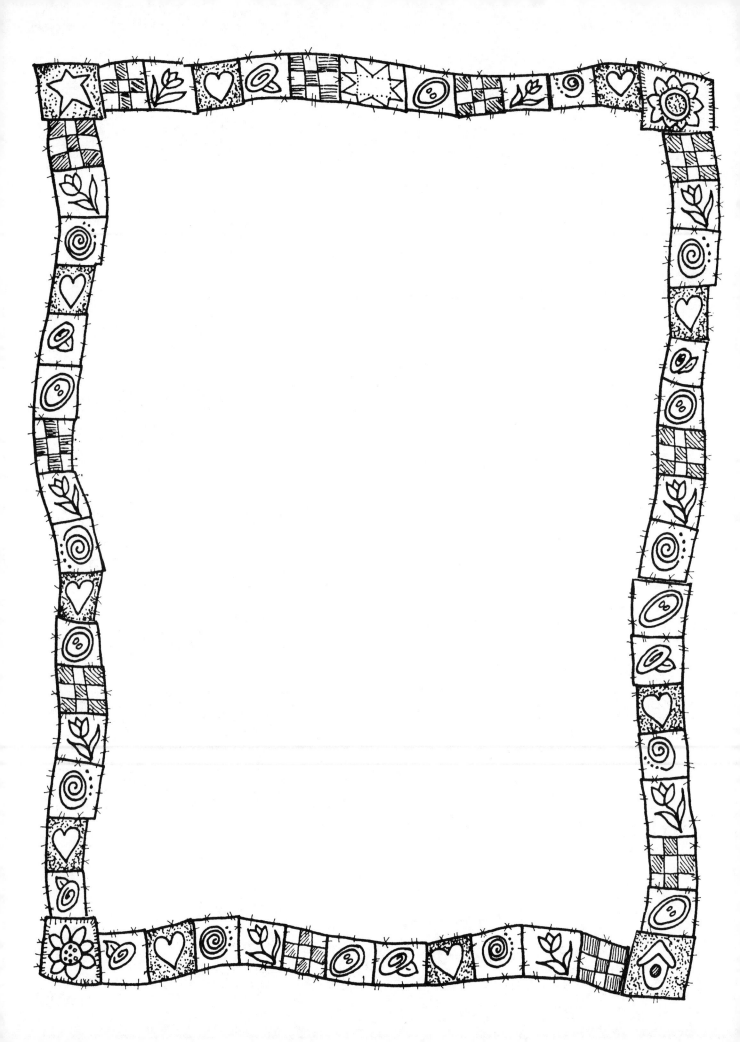

A gift made by hand is a gift from the heart

Crafts Forever
Housework Whenever

Computer Wizard!

I only craft on days that end with "y"

HELP: I'm online and I can't QUIT

If it doesn't move — paint it!

ATTENTION:
WE INTERRUPT THIS MARRIAGE FOR CRAFT SHOW SEASON

UPGRADE:
Take out old bugs
Put in new bugs

I know you can make it But will you?

Creative clutter is better than idle neatness

Behind every creative person is a closet full of ideas

I'm creative
You can't expect me to be neat too!

I'm not unorganized,
I just need a bigger Craft Room

45

Enter with a happy heart

TOGETHER IS A WONDERFUL PLACE TO BE

Happiness is homemade

Love is so Nice To Come Home To

Home is where you hang your heart

No matter what
No matter where
It's always home
If love is there

Within this home may love abide and warm all those who step inside

East or West Home is best.

Home is where your ♥ is

LOVE IS HOMESPUN

A house is made of Wood and Stone but only Love can make it a home

Our Best Memories Are Homemade

47

Good Times & Friends Dear
Forever Welcome Here

HOME

Welcome to Grand Central Station

There's no place like home.

A man's Home is his Castle... until the Queen Arrives

Love Nest

Home Tweet Home

Love Lives in Cottages As Well as Castles
- English Proverb

Home is where you plant yourself

Here may you live life at its best
May you find true comfort and rest.
- 1800 English Sampler

Bachelor Pad Enter at Your Own Risk

A happy home is where both mates think they got better than they deserve

49

Our Family Shares Everything... Even Chores!

| Chore | ✳ | Name | ✳ | Completed |

Bless Those Who Clean Up

HOUSE RULES
1. MOM'S THE BOSS
2. SEE RULE #1

"M" is for MOTHER NOT MAID

Dull women have Immaculate Houses

HOUSEWORK MAKES ME WANT TO CROAK!

BATHROOM RULES
Wash
Brush
Floss
&
Flush

 Housework makes you homely.

This house is protected by killer dust bunnies

Dust is a protective cover for furniture

Too much housework can cause brain damage

HELP WANTED:
Everyone in this house is qualified.

51

Bless This Mess

Four Letter
Dirty Words

Wash,
Cook,
Iron
&
Dust

MOM'S TAXI

Swiss Army Wife

Is there life after laundry?

Just say NO to crafts Housework

I clean house every other day. This is not the other day.

Why does everyone in the universe think MOMS know where everything is? Because no one but MOMS put anything away

Tornado Zone

Where are all the spoons? With all the lost socks

This House Is Clean Enough To Be Healthy... Dirty Enough To Be Happy!

If you write in the dust... please don't date it.

Dust is just a country accent.

A woman's work is never done — because she's never home

Cross my country heart ♡

53

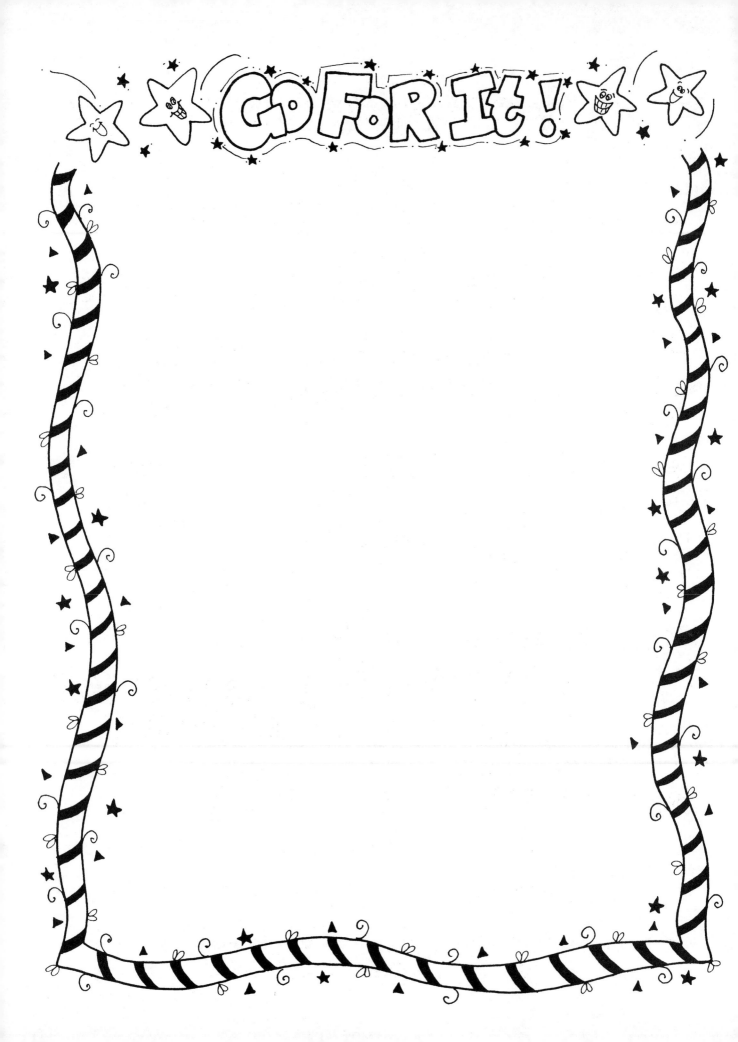

Aim for your Star

Those Who Reach Touch the Stars

BELIEVE TO ACHIEVE

He turns not back who is bound to a star

-Leonardo Da Vinci

The city of happiness is in the state of mind

When things look down....look up

The best way to be SPECIAL....
is to be YOURSELF!

Ideas never work unless we do

For every problem there is an opportunity.

Every dream and goal in me are all inspired by your love and loyalty ~

Enjoy the Journey

Look for life's greatest treasures
in life's simplest pleasures

Purr-fectly Wonderful

STOP to smell the flowers

The gift of happiness belongs to those who unwrap it

Inspiration

share the warmth of your smile

Dreams are a wish your heart makes

smile it's catching

FOLLOW YOUR DREAMS

Commit random acts of kindness and senseless acts of beauty.

A smile adds a great deal to one's face value

All the wonders you seek are within yourself
- Sir Thomas Brown

If there seems to be no bright side in your life polish up your dark side

From a Little Spark May Burst a Mighty Flame
- Dante

Plant Goals & Harvest Dreams

Paint Your own rainbows in life

57

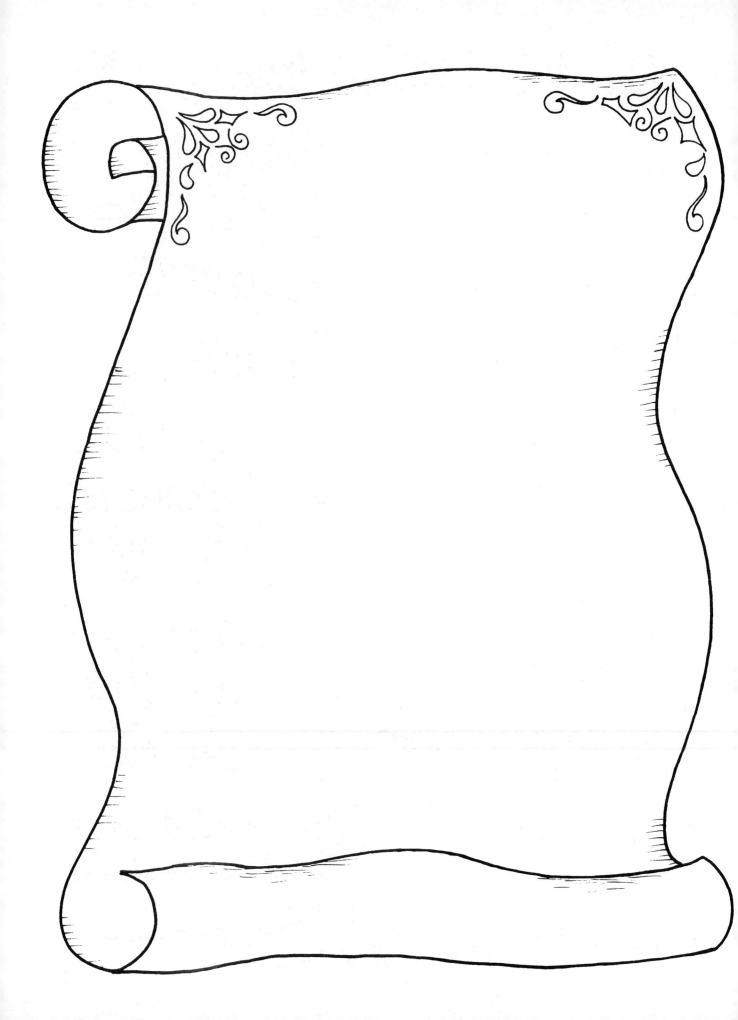

Dare to be different

Never let the fear of striking out get in your way
- Babe Ruth

DARE to Dream

Anyone can leap with a little faith

Be an Original not a copy

Live Well Laugh Often Love Much

There is never a wrong time to do the right thing

The best preparation for tomorrow... is the best use of today

Think BIG

Put Your Heart In It

It's not how much you have. It's how you enjoy it.

Make the most of yourself for that is all there is of you

Make stepping stones out of stumbling stones

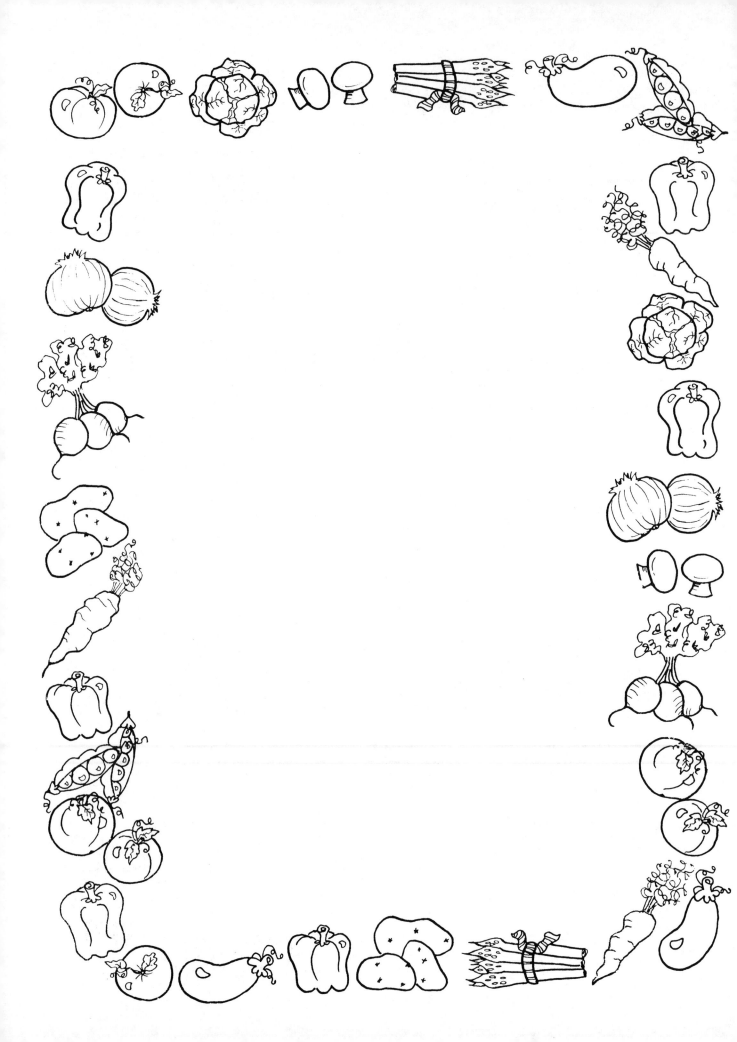

My Kitchen & Me Welcome Thee

A Messy Kitchen is a Happy Place This one is DELIRIOUS!

KISS THE COOK

MOM'S CAFE
THOSE WHO TIP IN HELP & HUGS EAT FREE

I made my favorite thing for Supper... a reservation

Just say No! to cooking.

Season Everything With Love

This Kitchen is Self Serve

Miracles Served Here

No Matter Where I Serve My guests They Seem to like My Kitchen Best

Life is Tea-rrific!

Keep This Kitchen Clean EAT OUT

COMPLAINTS to the COOK CAN BE HAZARDOUS TO YOUR HEALTH

I don't do mornings

Is it coffee yet?

61

You're Beautiful Inside & Out

Love

Having you so far away, adds new meaning to the word

L O N G I T U D E

Thank you for all you are
and what you'll always be,
so darn easy to love.......
it just comes naturally

I Want To Be
By Your Side
In The Sunshine
And The Rain

The world is
a nicer place
because of you

I want to shower you
with a million kisses

Together
we make
Magic

Bee my
Sweet
Valentine

Hypnotized
by Love

We'll make it to all those
dreams we share.
Because we make a
truly perfect pair.

True love is.....

Friendship set on fire
- French Proverb

Love Ya!

Dance Through Life With Me
The Best is Yet To Be

Love Lives in Happy Hearts

All things grow with love

Let all that you do be done in Love.

If thoughts of you made stars appear new galaxies would unfold here -

Letters Mingle Souls

Joy shared is Joy doubled

Miles can't separate hearts that care

This gift is all wrapped and tied, With wishes of love all tucked inside....

Love doesn't make the world go around... but it sure makes the ride worthwhile

Love is a present we can give every single day

Life is for Living Love is for Giving.

The best gifts are tied with heartstrings

Love is the glue that holds the world together.

Love is Love Reflected

Over The Hill And Picking Up Speed

Happy 29th... again?

" The older the violin
The sweeter the music "

It's not a matter of growing old
It's getting old if you stop growing

In a dream,
you are
never 80
- Anne Sexton

Be nice to your children,
for they will choose your rest home
- Phyliss Diller

**Over the hill...
and picking up speed**

I'm not young enough
to know everthing

YOUNG AT HEART
slightly older in other places

Age,
doesnt
matter...
unless
you're
CHEESE!

In DOG years...
I'm DEAD

NATURAL
AGING
WOMAN

You're only young once.
But you can be immature.
FOREVER

Wrinkles are not so bad,
they just show where
smiles have been

BETTER TO BE OVER THE HILL...
THAN UNDER IT!

I'm not aging.....
I'm marinating.

67

a picture perfect moment

WILD THING

It's Party Time!

You take the Cake

An Occassion for a Royal Celebration

Belle of the Ball

You're my honey Bear

Hail to the Birthday King

PLEASE be Patient... I'm a work in Progress

Perfect Pals

Simply adorable

2 cute 4 words

made to treasure

69

Roughing It in the Wild

Diagnosis: Cabin Fever or (Camping)

Beach Bums

This must be Paradise

ON THE ROAD AGAIN

Catch the Wave

BOYS SURE LOVE THEIR TOYS

Girls Night Out

Words can't express our love for you. This moment captures why its true.

A Milestone To Remember~

The Cat's Meow

Who Said Fairytails Don't Come True?

We Interrupt This Marriage For Baseball Season or (Football)

It's Baseball Batty Season

Old Soccer Players Never Die They Just Lose Their Kick

Tennis is my racket

Old skiers never die they just go downhill

Golf Stories Told Here (slightly exaggerated)

Life is a Game But Golf is Serious!

Golf is a steady diet of greens

18

Reel Fishin' Pals

I golf... therefore I lie

When I die throw me in a lake so my husband will fish for ME!

Gone fishin' Just for the halibut

TALL FISH TALES TOLD HERE

Hooked on fishin'

Good things come to those who bait

Old fishermen never die they just smell that way

The only thing working on this ol' boat is the Owner

73

Anytime is stitchin time

Stitching Quilts

Friendships are sewn...
one stitch at a time

Life is a patchwork of
FRIENDS

You're SEW SPECIAL

Mending and stitching
with Mr. Wind blowing
the days pass quickly
while I am sewing

From my hands
To your heart

You can always count on
X - Stitchers ♥

Blessed are the piecemakers!

Love is the thread that binds us

Quilting with a friend
will keep you in stitches

Behind every sewan
is a huge pile
of fabric

Quilters never grow old,
They just go to pieces.

Quilters never
cut corners

I ♥ SEWING and HAVE PLENTY of MATERIAL WITNESSES

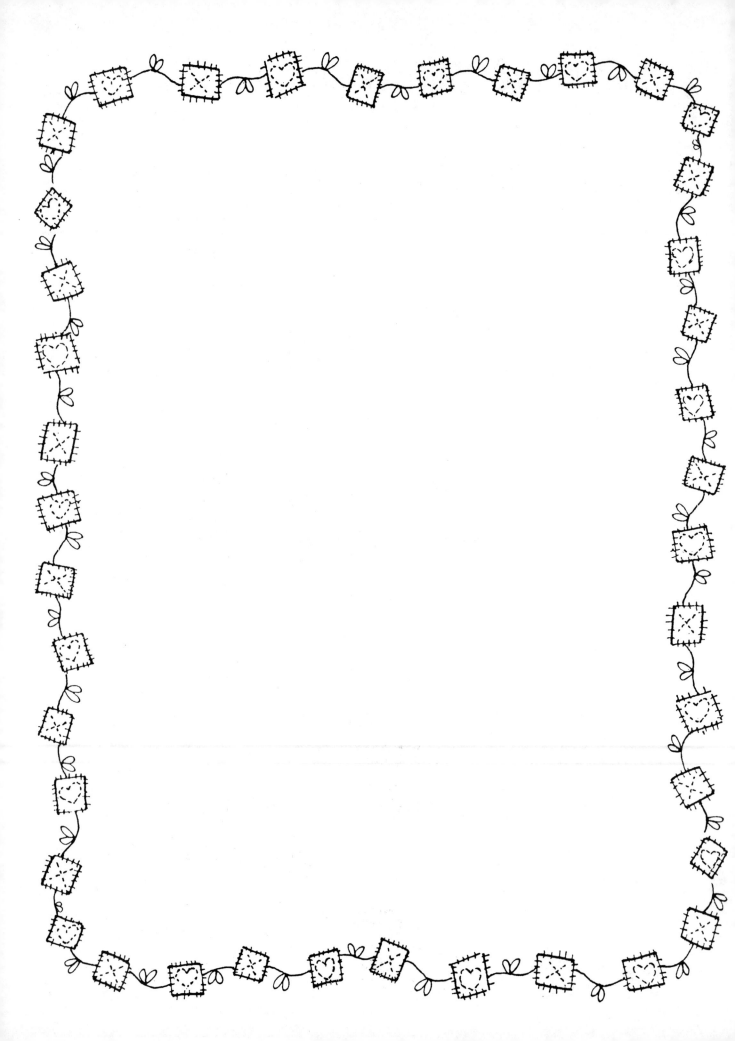

My Soul Is Fed By Needle & Thread

Stitchin' & Quiltin'

In the crazy quilt of life, I'm glad you're in my block of friends

A quilt is something you make To keep someone you love... WARM

I'm in therapy & SEWING is cheaper than a psychiatrist

A quilt is a blanket of Love

When life gives you scraps Make quilts

Good friends are like quilts They never lose their warmth

Quilts are like friends— a great source of comfort

Memories are stitched with love

Touch these scissors and die!

Sew much fabric Sew little time

Sewing and Crafts fill my days not to mention the livingroom, bedroom and closets

She who dies with the most fabric... WINS!

Aa Bb Cc Dd Ee Ff Gg Hh

Ii Jj Kk Ll Mm Nn Oo Pp

Qq Rr Ss Tt Uu Vv Ww Xx Yy Zz

Teachers Touch the Future

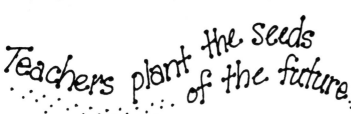

Teachers plant the seeds of the future

Children shouldn't be molded instead tenderly unfolded

Teaching is a work of heart

Experience is the Best Teacher but the Tuition is Costly

2 Teach is
2 Touch lives
———————
4 Ever

MANY CAN TEACH, ONLY A SPECIAL FEW CAN REACH

Look WHAT I DID AT SCHOOL!

Teachers have CLASS

YOU REALLY MEASURE UP!

GRADUATE You're full of... Potential!

Teaching is the profession... that creates all others.

If you can read this — thank a teacher!

Honey

You're beary sweet

Honey

Love makes all things BEARABLE !

Teddies

Teddy bears are stuffed  with dreams and memories

My teddy is old and full of tatters, but he loves me back and that's all that matters

Beauty is in the eyes of the "bear" holder

YOU'RE BEARY SPECIAL

YOU make me so Beary Beary Happy

Honey

Bear Hugs for My Honey

Beary Best Friends

Wanted: child to LOVE Age 1~101

LOVE ME LOVE MY TEDDY BEAR

♥ Love breeds teddy bears
Teddy bears breed love. ♥

Sometimes love is a little heart to bear ✿

ReMem-BeAR ... I Wuv You BEARY Much

Aa Bb Cc Dd Ee

Ff Gg Hh Ii Jj

Kk Ll Mm Nn Oo

Pp Qq Rr Ss Tt Uu

Vv Ww Xx Yy Zz

1 2 3 4 5 6 7 8 9 0

Alphabets

Aa Bb Cc Dd Ee Ff Gg
Hh Ii Jj Kk Ll Mm Nn
Ss Tt Uu Oo Pp Qq Rr
Vv Ww Xx Yy Zz
1 2 3 4 5 6 7 8 9 0

Aa Bb Cc Dd Ee Ff Gg Hh Ii
Jj Kk Ll Mm Nn Oo Pp Qq Rr
Ss Tt Uu Vv Ww Xx Yy Zz.
1 2 3 4 5 6 7 8 9 0

85

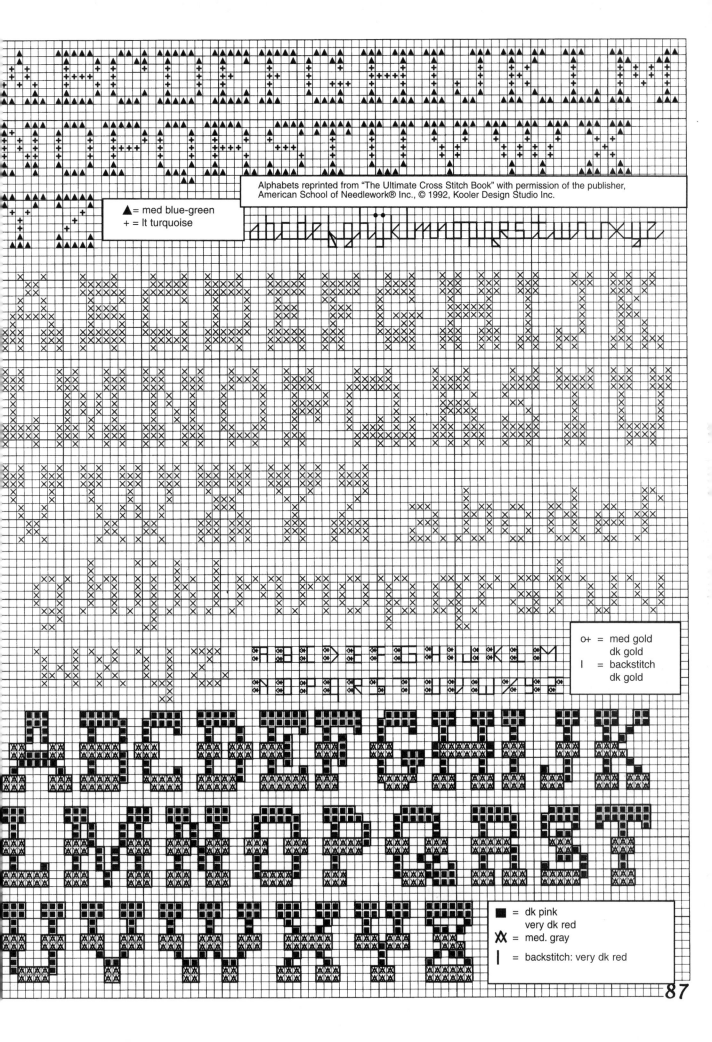

▲ = med blue-green
+ = lt turquoise

o+ = med gold
      dk gold
I = backstitch
     dk gold

■ = dk pink
    very dk red
✗ = med. gray
I = backstitch: very dk red

HOW TO ADD MORE JOY TO LIFE

LOOK for the POSITIVE in EVERYTHING

Show those You Love; Lots of Love

Learn to Forgive

Learn to Relax

LOOK for More Reasons to LAUGH

Feed Your creativity

Own a Lovable Pet

Look after Your Body & Mind

Discover New Friends & New Experiences

Cherish Your Old Friends & Old Memories

Eat Delicious Food that's Good for You

Use Your Favorite Dishes (paper plates?)

Tantalize all Your senses often

Do what YOU LOVE and get Paid for it

Practice Random Acts of KINDNESS

Believe in Miracles

Cuddle a Baby

Write or call someone You care about

Own some COZY Pajamas

Have more Indoor & Outdoor Picnics

FOllow YOUR RAINBOWS

Nurture Your Spirituality

LEND SOMEONE a HAND

Sing in the car & Dance through Life

Cultivate a Gratitude Attitude

GO for the Goals You Really Want

Find Someone to PLaY With

Start a Journal or Paint a Picture

Give & Get More HUGS

Display Your Favorite Photographs

Celebrate for BiG & Little Reasons

LOOK for Angels & Fairies

Find ways to Simplify Your LIFE

Don't Give Guilt Trips or Have Them

Have More Bubble Baths

Stop to Smell the Flowers

Find Your PASSION & ENJOY iT

Create More Heartwarming Moments

COUNT Your BLESSINGS Everyday

Joy is Best kept when Given away

By Sandy Redburn